The Vaudois and other p

Part 1 From Volume I of The Works of
John Greenleaf Whittier

John Greenleaf Whittier

Alpha Editions

This edition published in 2024

ISBN : 9789362922236

Design and Setting By
Alpha Editions
www.alphaedis.com
Email - info@alphaedis.com

As per information held with us this book is in Public Domain.
This book is a reproduction of an important historical work. Alpha Editions uses the best technology to reproduce historical work in the same manner it was first published to preserve its original nature. Any marks or number seen are left intentionally to preserve its true form.

Contents

PROEM .... - 1 -
INTRODUCTION .... - 2 -
NARRATIVE AND LEGENDARY POEMS .... - 4 -
THE FEMALE MARTYR. .... - 6 -
THE DEMON OF THE STUDY. .... - 11 -
THE FOUNTAIN. .... - 14 -
PENTUCKET. .... - 18 -
THE NORSEMEN. .... - 21 -
FUNERAL TREE OF THE SOKOKIS. .... - 25 -
ST. JOHN. .... - 28 -
THE CYPRESS-TREE OF CEYLON. .... - 32 -
THE EXILES. .... - 35 -
THE KNIGHT OF ST. JOHN. .... - 42 -
THE NEW WIFE AND THE OLD. .... - 51 -

PROEM

I LOVE the old melodious lays
Which softly melt the ages through,
The songs of Spenser's golden days,
Arcadian Sidney's silvery phrase,
Sprinkling our noon of time with freshest morning dew.

Yet, vainly in my quiet hours
To breathe their marvellous notes I try;
I feel them, as the leaves and flowers
In silence feel the dewy showers,
And drink with glad, still lips the blessing of the sky.

The rigor of a frozen clime,
The harshness of an untaught ear,
The jarring words of one whose rhyme
Beat often Labor's hurried time,
Or Duty's rugged march through storm and strife, are here.

Of mystic beauty, dreamy grace,
No rounded art the lack supplies;
Unskilled the subtle lines to trace,
Or softer shades of Nature's face,
I view her common forms with unanointed eyes.

Nor mine the seer-like power to show
The secrets of the heart and mind;
To drop the plummet-line below
Our common world of joy and woe,
A more intense despair or brighter hope to find.

Yet here at least an earnest sense
Of human right and weal is shown;
A hate of tyranny intense,
And hearty in its vehemence,
As if my brother's pain and sorrow were my own.

O Freedom! if to me belong
Nor mighty Milton's gift divine,
Nor Marvell's wit and graceful song,
Still with a love as deep and strong
As theirs, I lay, like them, my best gifts on thy shrine.

AMESBURY, 11th mo., 1847.

INTRODUCTION

The edition of my poems published in 1857 contained the following note by way of preface:—

"In these volumes, for the first time, a complete collection of my poetical writings has been made. While it is satisfactory to know that these scattered children of my brain have found a home, I cannot but regret that I have been unable, by reason of illness, to give that attention to their revision and arrangement, which respect for the opinions of others and my own afterthought and experience demand.

"That there are pieces in this collection which I would 'willingly let die,' I am free to confess. But it is now too late to disown them, and I must submit to the inevitable penalty of poetical as well as other sins. There are others, intimately connected with the author's life and times, which owe their tenacity of vitality to the circumstances under which they were written, and the events by which they were suggested.

"The long poem of Mogg Megone was in a great measure composed in early life; and it is scarcely necessary to say that its subject is not such as the writer would have chosen at any subsequent period."

After a lapse of thirty years since the above was written, I have been requested by my publishers to make some preparation for a new and revised edition of my poems. I cannot flatter myself that I have added much to the interest of the work beyond the correction of my own errors and those of the press, with the addition of a few heretofore unpublished pieces, and occasional notes of explanation which seemed necessary. I have made an attempt to classify the poems under a few general heads, and have transferred the long poem of Mogg Megone to the Appendix, with other specimens of my earlier writings. I have endeavored to affix the dates of composition or publication as far as possible.

In looking over these poems I have not been unmindful of occasional prosaic lines and verbal infelicities, but at this late day I have neither strength nor patience to undertake their correction.

Perhaps a word of explanation may be needed in regard to a class of poems written between the years 1832 and 1865. Of their defects from an artistic point of view it is not necessary to speak. They were the earnest and often vehement expression of the writer's thought and feeling at critical periods in the great conflict between Freedom and Slavery. They were written with no expectation that they would survive the occasions which called them forth: they were protests, alarm signals, trumpet-calls to action, words wrung from the writer's heart, forged at white heat, and of course lacking the finish and careful word-selection which reflection and patient brooding over them might have given. Such as they are, they belong to the history of the Anti-Slavery movement, and may serve as way-marks of its progress. If their language at times seems severe and harsh, the monstrous wrong of Slavery which provoked it must be its excuse, if any is needed. In attacking it, we did not measure our words. "It is," said Garrison, "a waste of politeness to be courteous to the devil." But in truth the contest was, in a great measure, an impersonal one,—hatred of slavery and not of slave-masters.

> "No common wrong provoked our zeal,
> The silken gauntlet which is thrown
> In such a quarrel rings like steel."

Even Thomas Jefferson, in his terrible denunciation of Slavery in the Notes on Virginia, says "It is impossible to be temperate and pursue the subject of Slavery." After the great contest was over, no class of the American people were more ready, with kind words and deprecation of harsh retaliation, to welcome back the revolted States than the Abolitionists; and none have since more heartily rejoiced at the fast increasing prosperity of the South.

Grateful for the measure of favor which has been accorded to my writings, I leave this edition with the public. It contains all that I care to re-publish, and some things which, had the matter of choice been left solely to myself, I should have omitted. J. G. W.

NARRATIVE AND LEGENDARY POEMS

THE VAUDOIS TEACHER.

This poem was suggested by the account given of the manner which the Waldenses disseminated their principles among the Catholic gentry. They gained access to the house through their occupation as peddlers of silks, jewels, and trinkets. "Having disposed of some of their goods," it is said by a writer who quotes the inquisitor Rainerus Sacco, "they cautiously intimated that they had commodities far more valuable than these, inestimable jewels, which they would show if they could be protected from the clergy. They would then give their purchasers a Bible or Testament; and thereby many were deluded into heresy." The poem, under the title Le Colporteur Vaudois, was translated into French by Professor G. de Felice, of Montauban, and further naturalized by Professor Alexandre Rodolphe Vinet, who quoted it in his lectures on French literature, afterwards published. It became familiar in this form to the Waldenses, who adopted it as a household poem. An American clergyman, J. C. Fletcher, frequently heard it when he was a student, about the year 1850, in the theological seminary at Geneva, Switzerland, but the authorship of the poem was unknown to those who used it. Twenty-five years later, Mr. Fletcher, learning the name of the author, wrote to the moderator of the Waldensian synod at La Tour, giving the information. At the banquet which closed the meeting of the synod, the moderator announced the fact, and was instructed in the name of the Waldensian church to write to me a letter of thanks. My letter, written in reply, was translated into Italian and printed throughout Italy.

"O LADY fair, these silks of mine
    are beautiful and rare,—
The richest web of the Indian loom, which beauty's
    queen might wear;
And my pearls are pure as thy own fair neck, with whose
    radiant light they vie;
I have brought them with me a weary way,—will my
    gentle lady buy?"

The lady smiled on the worn old man through the
    dark and clustering curls
Which veiled her brow, as she bent to view his
    silks and glittering pearls;
And she placed their price in the old man's hand
    and lightly turned away,
But she paused at the wanderer's earnest call,—
    "My gentle lady, stay!

"O lady fair, I have yet a gem which a purer
    lustre flings,
Than the diamond flash of the jewelled crown on
    the lofty brow of kings;
A wonderful pearl of exceeding price, whose virtue
    shall not decay,
Whose light shall be as a spell to thee and a
    blessing on thy way!"

The lady glanced at the mirroring steel where her
    form of grace was seen,
Where her eye shone clear, and her dark locks
    waved their clasping pearls between;
"Bring forth thy pearl of exceeding worth, thou
    traveller gray and old,
And name the price of thy precious gem, and my
    page shall count thy gold."

The cloud went off from the pilgrim's brow, as a
    small and meagre book,
Unchased with gold or gem of cost, from his
    folding robe he took!
"Here, lady fair, is the pearl of price, may it prove
    as such to thee
Nay, keep thy gold—I ask it not, for the word of
    God is free!"

The hoary traveller went his way, but the gift he
    left behind
Hath had its pure and perfect work on that high-
    born maiden's mind,
And she hath turned from the pride of sin to the
    lowliness of truth,
And given her human heart to God in its beautiful
    hour of youth

And she hath left the gray old halls, where an evil faith had power, The courtly knights of her father's train, and the maidens of her bower; And she hath gone to the Vaudois vales by lordly feet untrod, Where the poor and needy of earth are rich in the perfect love of God! 1830.

THE FEMALE MARTYR.

Mary G———-, aged eighteen, a "Sister of Charity," died in one of our Atlantic cities, during the prevalence of the Indian cholera, while in voluntary attendance upon the sick.

"BRING out your dead!" The midnight street
Heard and gave back the hoarse, low call;
Harsh fell the tread of hasty feet,
Glanced through the dark the coarse white sheet,
Her coffin and her pall.
"What—only one!" the brutal hack-man said,
As, with an oath, he spurned away the dead.

How sunk the inmost hearts of all,
As rolled that dead-cart slowly by,
With creaking wheel and harsh hoof-fall!
The dying turned him to the wall,
To hear it and to die!
Onward it rolled; while oft its driver stayed,
And hoarsely clamored, "Ho! bring out your dead."

It paused beside the burial-place;
"Toss in your load!" and it was done.
With quick hand and averted face,
Hastily to the grave's embrace
They cast them, one by one,
Stranger and friend, the evil and the just,
Together trodden in the churchyard dust.

And thou, young martyr! thou wast there;
No white-robed sisters round thee trod,
Nor holy hymn, nor funeral prayer
Rose through the damp and noisome air,
Giving thee to thy God;
Nor flower, nor cross, nor hallowed taper gave
Grace to the dead, and beauty to the grave!

Yet, gentle sufferer! there shall be,
In every heart of kindly feeling,
A rite as holy paid to thee
As if beneath the convent-tree
Thy sisterhood were kneeling,
At vesper hours, like sorrowing angels, keeping
Their tearful watch around thy place of sleeping.

For thou wast one in whom the light
Of Heaven's own love was kindled well;
Enduring with a martyr's might,
Through weary day and wakeful night,
Far more than words may tell
Gentle, and meek, and lowly, and unknown,
Thy mercies measured by thy God alone!

Where manly hearts were failing, where
The throngful street grew foul with death,
O high-souled martyr! thou wast there,
Inhaling, from the loathsome air,
Poison with every breath.
Yet shrinking not from offices of dread
For the wrung dying, and the unconscious dead.

And, where the sickly taper shed
Its light through vapors, damp, confined,
Hushed as a seraph's fell thy tread,
A new Electra by the bed
Of suffering human-kind!
Pointing the spirit, in its dark dismay,
To that pure hope which fadeth not away.

Innocent teacher of the high
And holy mysteries of Heaven!
How turned to thee each glazing eye,
In mute and awful sympathy,
As thy low prayers were given;
And the o'er-hovering Spoiler wore, the while,
An angel's features, a deliverer's smile!

A blessed task! and worthy one
Who, turning from the world, as thou,
Before life's pathway had begun
To leave its spring-time flower and sun,
Had sealed her early vow;
Giving to God her beauty and her youth,
Her pure affections and her guileless truth.

Earth may not claim thee. Nothing here
Could be for thee a meet reward;
Thine is a treasure far more dear
Eye hath not seen it, nor the ear
Of living mortal heard

The joys prepared, the promised bliss above,
The holy presence of Eternal Love!

Sleep on in peace. The earth has not
A nobler name than thine shall be.
The deeds by martial manhood wrought,
The lofty energies of thought,
The fire of poesy,
These have but frail and fading honors; thine
Shall Time unto Eternity consign.

Yea, and when thrones shall crumble down,
And human pride and grandeur fall,
The herald's line of long renown,
The mitre and the kingly crown,—
Perishing glories all!
The pure devotion of thy generous heart
Shall live in Heaven, of which it was a part.
1833.

EXTRACT FROM "A NEW ENGLAND LEGEND."
(Originally a part of the author's Moll Pitcher.)

How has New England's romance fled,
Even as a vision of the morning!
Its rites foredone, its guardians dead,
Its priestesses, bereft of dread,
Waking the veriest urchin's scorning!
Gone like the Indian wizard's yell
And fire-dance round the magic rock,
Forgotten like the Druid's spell
At moonrise by his holy oak!
No more along the shadowy glen
Glide the dim ghosts of murdered men;
No more the unquiet churchyard dead
Glimpse upward from their turfy bed,
Startling the traveller, late and lone;
As, on some night of starless weather,
They silently commune together,
Each sitting on his own head-stone
The roofless house, decayed, deserted,
Its living tenants all departed,
No longer rings with midnight revel
Of witch, or ghost, or goblin evil;
No pale blue flame sends out its flashes

Through creviced roof and shattered sashes!
The witch-grass round the hazel spring
May sharply to the night-air sing,
But there no more shall withered hags
Refresh at ease their broomstick nags,
Or taste those hazel-shadowed waters
As beverage meet for Satan's daughters;
No more their mimic tones be heard,
The mew of cat, the chirp of bird,
Shrill blending with the hoarser laughter
Of the fell demon following after!
The cautious goodman nails no more
A horseshoe on his outer door,
Lest some unseemly hag should fit
To his own mouth her bridle-bit;
The goodwife's churn no more refuses
Its wonted culinary uses
Until, with heated needle burned,
The witch has to her place returned!
Our witches are no longer old
And wrinkled beldames, Satan-sold,
But young and gay and laughing creatures,
With the heart's sunshine on their features;
Their sorcery—the light which dances
Where the raised lid unveils its glances;
Or that low-breathed and gentle tone,
The music of Love's twilight hours,
Soft, dream-like, as a fairy's moan
Above her nightly closing flowers,
Sweeter than that which sighed of yore
Along the charmed Ausonian shore!
Even she, our own weird heroine,
Sole Pythoness of ancient Lynn,'
Sleeps calmly where the living laid her;
And the wide realm of sorcery,
Left by its latest mistress free,
Hath found no gray and skilled invader.
So—perished Albion's "glammarye,"
With him in Melrose Abbey sleeping,
His charmed torch beside his knee,
That even the dead himself might see
The magic scroll within his keeping.
And now our modern Yankee sees

Nor omens, spells, nor mysteries;
And naught above, below, around,
Of life or death, of sight or sound,
Whate'er its nature, form, or look,
Excites his terror or surprise,
All seeming to his knowing eyes
Familiar as his "catechise,"
Or "Webster's Spelling-Book."
1833.

THE DEMON OF THE STUDY.

THE Brownie sits in the Scotchman's room,
And eats his meat and drinks his ale,
And beats the maid with her unused broom,
And the lazy lout with his idle flail;
But he sweeps the floor and threshes the corn,
And hies him away ere the break of dawn.

The shade of Denmark fled from the sun,
And the Cocklane ghost from the barn-loft cheer,
The fiend of Faust was a faithful one,
Agrippa's demon wrought in fear,
And the devil of Martin Luther sat
By the stout monk's side in social chat.

The Old Man of the Sea, on the neck of him
Who seven times crossed the deep,
Twined closely each lean and withered limb,
Like the nightmare in one's sleep.
But he drank of the wine, and Sindbad cast
The evil weight from his back at last.

But the demon that cometh day by day
To my quiet room and fireside nook,
Where the casement light falls dim and gray
On faded painting and ancient book,
Is a sorrier one than any whose names
Are chronicled well by good King James.

No bearer of burdens like Caliban,
No runner of errands like Ariel,
He comes in the shape of a fat old man,
Without rap of knuckle or pull of bell;
And whence he comes, or whither he goes,
I know as I do of the wind which blows.

A stout old man with a greasy hat
Slouched heavily down to his dark, red nose,
And two gray eyes enveloped in fat,
Looking through glasses with iron bows.
Read ye, and heed ye, and ye who can,
Guard well your doors from that old man!

He comes with a careless "How d' ye do?"
And seats himself in my elbow-chair;

And my morning paper and pamphlet new
Fall forthwith under his special care,
And he wipes his glasses and clears his throat,
And, button by button, unfolds his coat.

And then he reads from paper and book,
In a low and husky asthmatic tone,
With the stolid sameness of posture and look
Of one who reads to himself alone;
And hour after hour on my senses come
That husky wheeze and that dolorous hum.

The price of stocks, the auction sales,
The poet's song and the lover's glee,
The horrible murders, the seaboard gales,
The marriage list, and the jeu d'esprit,
All reach my ear in the self-same tone,—
I shudder at each, but the fiend reads on!

Oh, sweet as the lapse of water at noon
O'er the mossy roots of some forest tree,
The sigh of the wind in the woods of June,
Or sound of flutes o'er a moonlight sea,
Or the low soft music, perchance, which seems
To float through the slumbering singer's dreams,

So sweet, so dear is the silvery tone,
Of her in whose features I sometimes look,
As I sit at eve by her side alone,
And we read by turns, from the self-same book,
Some tale perhaps of the olden time,
Some lover's romance or quaint old rhyme.

Then when the story is one of woe,—
Some prisoner's plaint through his dungeon-bar,
Her blue eye glistens with tears, and low
Her voice sinks down like a moan afar;
And I seem to hear that prisoner's wail,
And his face looks on me worn and pale.

And when she reads some merrier song,
Her voice is glad as an April bird's,
And when the tale is of war and wrong,
A trumpet's summons is in her words,
And the rush of the hosts I seem to hear,
And see the tossing of plume and spear!

Oh, pity me then, when, day by day,
The stout fiend darkens my parlor door;
And reads me perchance the self-same lay
Which melted in music, the night before,
From lips as the lips of Hylas sweet,
And moved like twin roses which zephyrs meet!

I cross my floor with a nervous tread,
I whistle and laugh and sing and shout,
I flourish my cane above his head,
And stir up the fire to roast him out;
I topple the chairs, and drum on the pane,
And press my hands on my ears, in vain!

I've studied Glanville and James the wise,
And wizard black-letter tomes which treat
Of demons of every name and size
Which a Christian man is presumed to meet,
But never a hint and never a line
Can I find of a reading fiend like mine.

I've crossed the Psalter with Brady and Tate,
And laid the Primer above them all,
I've nailed a horseshoe over the grate,
And hung a wig to my parlor wall
Once worn by a learned Judge, they say,
At Salem court in the witchcraft day!

"Conjuro te, sceleratissime,
Abire ad tuum locum!"—still
Like a visible nightmare he sits by me,—
The exorcism has lost its skill;
And I hear again in my haunted room
The husky wheeze and the dolorous hum!

Ah! commend me to Mary Magdalen
With her sevenfold plagues, to the wandering Jew,
To the terrors which haunted Orestes when
The furies his midnight curtains drew,
But charm him off, ye who charm him can,
That reading demon, that fat old man!
1835.

THE FOUNTAIN.

On the declivity of a hill in Salisbury, Essex County, is a fountain of clear water, gushing from the very roots of a venerable oak. It is about two miles from the junction of the Powow River with the Merrimac.

TRAVELLER! on thy journey toiling
By the swift Powow,
With the summer sunshine falling
On thy heated brow,
Listen, while all else is still,
To the brooklet from the hill.

Wild and sweet the flowers are blowing
By that streamlet's side,
And a greener verdure showing
Where its waters glide,
Down the hill-slope murmuring on,
Over root and mossy stone.

Where yon oak his broad arms flingeth
O'er the sloping hill,
Beautiful and freshly springeth
That soft-flowing rill,
Through its dark roots wreathed and bare,
Gushing up to sun and air.

Brighter waters sparkled never
In that magic well,
Of whose gift of life forever
Ancient legends tell,
In the lonely desert wasted,
And by mortal lip untasted.

Waters which the proud Castilian
Sought with longing eyes,
Underneath the bright pavilion
Of the Indian skies,
Where his forest pathway lay
Through the blooms of Florida.

Years ago a lonely stranger,
With the dusky brow
Of the outcast forest-ranger,
Crossed the swift Powow,

And betook him to the rill
And the oak upon the hill.

O'er his face of moody sadness
For an instant shone
Something like a gleam of gladness,
As he stooped him down
To the fountain's grassy side,
And his eager thirst supplied.

With the oak its shadow throwing
O'er his mossy seat,
And the cool, sweet waters flowing
Softly at his feet,
Closely by the fountain's rim
That lone Indian seated him.

Autumn's earliest frost had given
To the woods below
Hues of beauty, such as heaven
Lendeth to its bow;
And the soft breeze from the west
Scarcely broke their dreamy rest.

Far behind was Ocean striving
With his chains of sand;
Southward, sunny glimpses giving,
'Twixt the swells of land,
Of its calm and silvery track,
Rolled the tranquil Merrimac.

Over village, wood, and meadow
Gazed that stranger man,
Sadly, till the twilight shadow
Over all things ran,
Save where spire and westward pane
Flashed the sunset back again.

Gazing thus upon the dwelling
Of his warrior sires,
Where no lingering trace was telling
Of their wigwam fires,
Who the gloomy thoughts might know
Of that wandering child of woe?

Naked lay, in sunshine glowing,
Hills that once had stood

Down their sides the shadows throwing
Of a mighty wood,
Where the deer his covert kept,
And the eagle's pinion swept!

Where the birch canoe had glided
Down the swift Powow,
Dark and gloomy bridges strided
Those clear waters now;
And where once the beaver swam,
Jarred the wheel and frowned the dam.

For the wood-bird's merry singing,
And the hunter's cheer,
Iron clang and hammer's ringing
Smote upon his ear;
And the thick and sullen smoke
From the blackened forges broke.

Could it be his fathers ever
Loved to linger here?
These bare hills, this conquered river,—
Could they hold them dear,
With their native loveliness
Tamed and tortured into this?

Sadly, as the shades of even
Gathered o'er the hill,
While the western half of heaven
Blushed with sunset still,
From the fountain's mossy seat
Turned the Indian's weary feet.

Year on year hath flown forever,
But he came no more
To the hillside on the river
Where he came before.
But the villager can tell
Of that strange man's visit well.

And the merry children, laden
With their fruits or flowers,
Roving boy and laughing maiden,
In their school-day hours,
Love the simple tale to tell

Of the Indian and his well.
1837

PENTUCKET.

The village of Haverhill, on the Merrimac, called by the Indians Pentucket, was for nearly seventeen years a frontier town, and during thirty years endured all the horrors of savage warfare. In the year 1708, a combined body of French and Indians, under the command of De Chaillons, and Hertel de Rouville, the famous and bloody sacker of Deerfield, made an attack upon the village, which at that time contained only thirty houses. Sixteen of the villagers were massacred, and a still larger number made prisoners. About thirty of the enemy also fell, among them Hertel de Rouville. The minister of the place, Benjamin Rolfe, was killed by a shot through his own door. In a paper entitled The Border War of 1708, published in my collection of Recreations and Miscellanies, I have given a prose narrative of the surprise of Haverhill.

How sweetly on the wood-girt town
The mellow light of sunset shone!
Each small, bright lake, whose waters still
Mirror the forest and the hill,
Reflected from its waveless breast
The beauty of a cloudless west,
Glorious as if a glimpse were given
Within the western gates of heaven,
Left, by the spirit of the star
Of sunset's holy hour, ajar!

Beside the river's tranquil flood
The dark and low-walled dwellings stood,
Where many a rood of open land
Stretched up and down on either hand,
With corn-leaves waving freshly green
The thick and blackened stumps between.
Behind, unbroken, deep and dread,
The wild, untravelled forest spread,
Back to those mountains, white and cold,
Of which the Indian trapper told,
Upon whose summits never yet
Was mortal foot in safety set.

Quiet and calm without a fear,
Of danger darkly lurking near,
The weary laborer left his plough,
The milkmaid carolled by her cow;

From cottage door and household hearth
Rose songs of praise, or tones of mirth.

At length the murmur died away,
And silence on that village lay.
—So slept Pompeii, tower and hall,
Ere the quick earthquake swallowed all,
Undreaming of the fiery fate
Which made its dwellings desolate.

Hours passed away. By moonlight sped
The Merrimac along his bed.
Bathed in the pallid lustre, stood
Dark cottage-wall and rock and wood,
Silent, beneath that tranquil beam,
As the hushed grouping of a dream.
Yet on the still air crept a sound,
No bark of fox, nor rabbit's bound,
Nor stir of wings, nor waters flowing,
Nor leaves in midnight breezes blowing.

Was that the tread of many feet,
Which downward from the hillside beat?
What forms were those which darkly stood
Just on the margin of the wood?—
Charred tree-stumps in the moonlight dim,
Or paling rude, or leafless limb?
No,—through the trees fierce eyeballs glowed,
Dark human forms in moonshine showed,
Wild from their native wilderness,
With painted limbs and battle-dress.

A yell the dead might wake to hear
Swelled on the night air, far and clear;
Then smote the Indian tomahawk
On crashing door and shattering lock;

Then rang the rifle-shot, and then
The shrill death-scream of stricken men,—
Sank the red axe in woman's brain,
And childhood's cry arose in vain.
Bursting through roof and window came,
Red, fast, and fierce, the kindled flame,
And blended fire and moonlight glared
On still dead men and scalp-knives bared.

The morning sun looked brightly through
The river willows, wet with dew.
No sound of combat filled the air,
No shout was heard, nor gunshot there;
Yet still the thick and sullen smoke
From smouldering ruins slowly broke;
And on the greensward many a stain,
And, here and there, the mangled slain,
Told how that midnight bolt had sped
Pentucket, on thy fated head.

Even now the villager can tell
Where Rolfe beside his hearthstone fell,
Still show the door of wasting oak,
Through which the fatal death-shot broke,
And point the curious stranger where
De Rouville's corse lay grim and bare;
Whose hideous head, in death still feared,
Bore not a trace of hair or beard;
And still, within the churchyard ground,
Heaves darkly up the ancient mound,
Whose grass-grown surface overlies
The victims of that sacrifice.
1838.

THE NORSEMEN.

In the early part of the present century, a fragment of a statue, rudely chiselled from dark gray stone, was found in the town of Bradford, on the Merrimac. Its origin must be left entirely to conjecture. The fact that the ancient Northmen visited the north-east coast of North America and probably New England, some centuries before the discovery of the western world by Columbus, is very generally admitted.

GIFT from the cold and silent Past!
A relic to the present cast,
Left on the ever-changing strand
Of shifting and unstable sand,
Which wastes beneath the steady chime
And beating of the waves of Time!
Who from its bed of primal rock
First wrenched thy dark, unshapely block?
Whose hand, of curious skill untaught,
Thy rude and savage outline wrought?

The waters of my native stream
Are glancing in the sun's warm beam;
From sail-urged keel and flashing oar
The circles widen to its shore;
And cultured field and peopled town
Slope to its willowed margin down.
Yet, while this morning breeze is bringing
The home-life sound of school-bells ringing,
And rolling wheel, and rapid jar
Of the fire-winged and steedless car,
And voices from the wayside near
Come quick and blended on my ear,—
A spell is in this old gray stone,
My thoughts are with the Past alone!

A change!—The steepled town no more
Stretches along the sail-thronged shore;
Like palace-domes in sunset's cloud,
Fade sun-gilt spire and mansion proud
Spectrally rising where they stood,
I see the old, primeval wood;
Dark, shadow-like, on either hand
I see its solemn waste expand;
It climbs the green and cultured hill,

It arches o'er the valley's rill,
And leans from cliff and crag to throw
Its wild arms o'er the stream below.
Unchanged, alone, the same bright river
Flows on, as it will flow forever
I listen, and I hear the low
Soft ripple where its waters go;
I hear behind the panther's cry,
The wild-bird's scream goes thrilling by,
And shyly on the river's brink
The deer is stooping down to drink.

But hark!—from wood and rock flung back,
What sound comes up the Merrimac?
What sea-worn barks are those which throw
The light spray from each rushing prow?
Have they not in the North Sea's blast
Bowed to the waves the straining mast?
Their frozen sails the low, pale sun
Of Thule's night has shone upon;
Flapped by the sea-wind's gusty sweep
Round icy drift, and headland steep.
Wild Jutland's wives and Lochlin's daughters
Have watched them fading o'er the waters,
Lessening through driving mist and spray,
Like white-winged sea-birds on their way!

Onward they glide,—and now I view
Their iron-armed and stalwart crew;
Joy glistens in each wild blue eye,
Turned to green earth and summer sky.
Each broad, seamed breast has cast aside
Its cumbering vest of shaggy hide;
Bared to the sun and soft warm air,
Streams back the Norsemen's yellow hair.
I see the gleam of axe and spear,
The sound of smitten shields I hear,
Keeping a harsh and fitting time
To Saga's chant, and Runic rhyme;
Such lays as Zetland's Scald has sung,
His gray and naked isles among;
Or muttered low at midnight hour
Round Odin's mossy stone of power.
The wolf beneath the Arctic moon

Has answered to that startling rune;
The Gael has heard its stormy swell,
The light Frank knows its summons well;
Iona's sable-stoled Culdee
Has heard it sounding o'er the sea,
And swept, with hoary beard and hair,
His altar's foot in trembling prayer.

'T is past,—the 'wildering vision dies
In darkness on my dreaming eyes
The forest vanishes in air,
Hill-slope and vale lie starkly bare;
I hear the common tread of men,
And hum of work-day life again;

The mystic relic seems alone
A broken mass of common stone;
And if it be the chiselled limb
Of Berserker or idol grim,
A fragment of Valhalla's Thor,
The stormy Viking's god of War,
Or Praga of the Runic lay,
Or love-awakening Siona,
I know not,—for no graven line,
Nor Druid mark, nor Runic sign,
Is left me here, by which to trace
Its name, or origin, or place.
Yet, for this vision of the Past,
This glance upon its darkness cast,
My spirit bows in gratitude
Before the Giver of all good,
Who fashioned so the human mind,
That, from the waste of Time behind,
A simple stone, or mound of earth,
Can summon the departed forth;
Quicken the Past to life again,
The Present lose in what hath been,
And in their primal freshness show
The buried forms of long ago.
As if a portion of that Thought
By which the Eternal will is wrought,
Whose impulse fills anew with breath
The frozen solitude of Death,
To mortal mind were sometimes lent,

To mortal musings sometimes sent,
To whisper-even when it seems
But Memory's fantasy of dreams—
Through the mind's waste of woe and sin,
Of an immortal origin!
1841.

FUNERAL TREE OF THE SOKOKIS.

Polan, chief of the Sokokis Indians of the country between Agamenticus and Casco Bay, was killed at Windham on Sebago Lake in the spring of 1756. After the whites had retired, the surviving Indians "swayed" or bent down a young tree until its roots were upturned, placed the body of their chief beneath it, then released the tree, which, in springing back to its old position, covered the grave. The Sokokis were early converts to the Catholic faith. Most of them, prior to the year 1756, had removed to the French settlements on the St. Francois.

AROUND Sebago's lonely lake
There lingers not a breeze to break
The mirror which its waters make.

The solemn pines along its shore,
The firs which hang its gray rocks o'er,
Are painted on its glassy floor.

The sun looks o'er, with hazy eye,
The snowy mountain-tops which lie
Piled coldly up against the sky.

Dazzling and white! save where the bleak,
Wild winds have bared some splintering peak,
Or snow-slide left its dusky streak.

Yet green are Saco's banks below,
And belts of spruce and cedar show,
Dark fringing round those cones of snow.

The earth hath felt the breath of spring,
Though yet on her deliverer's wing
The lingering frosts of winter cling.

Fresh grasses fringe the meadow-brooks,
And mildly from its sunny nooks
The blue eye of the violet looks.

And odors from the springing grass,
The sweet birch and the sassafras,
Upon the scarce-felt breezes pass.

Her tokens of renewing care
Hath Nature scattered everywhere,
In bud and flower, and warmer air.

But in their hour of bitterness,
What reek the broken Sokokis,
Beside their slaughtered chief, of this?

The turf's red stain is yet undried,
Scarce have the death-shot echoes died
Along Sebago's wooded side;

And silent now the hunters stand,
Grouped darkly, where a swell of land
Slopes upward from the lake's white sand.

Fire and the axe have swept it bare,
Save one lone beech, unclosing there
Its light leaves in the vernal air.

With grave, cold looks, all sternly mute,
They break the damp turf at its foot,
And bare its coiled and twisted root.

They heave the stubborn trunk aside,
The firm roots from the earth divide,—
The rent beneath yawns dark and wide.

And there the fallen chief is laid,
In tasselled garb of skins arrayed,
And girded with his wampum-braid.

The silver cross he loved is pressed
Beneath the heavy arms, which rest
Upon his scarred and naked breast.

'T is done: the roots are backward sent,
The beechen-tree stands up unbent,
The Indian's fitting monument!

When of that sleeper's broken race
Their green and pleasant dwelling-place,
Which knew them once, retains no trace;

Oh, long may sunset's light be shed
As now upon that beech's head,
A green memorial of the dead!

There shall his fitting requiem be,
In northern winds, that, cold and free,
Howl nightly in that funeral tree.

To their wild wail the waves which break
Forever round that lonely lake
A solemn undertone shall make!

And who shall deem the spot unblest,
Where Nature's younger children rest,
Lulled on their sorrowing mother's breast?

Deem ye that mother loveth less
These bronzed forms of the wilderness
She foldeth in her long caress?

As sweet o'er them her wild-flowers blow,
As if with fairer hair and brow
The blue-eyed Saxon slept below.

What though the places of their rest
No priestly knee hath ever pressed,—
No funeral rite nor prayer hath blessed?

What though the bigot's ban be there,
And thoughts of wailing and despair,
And cursing in the place of prayer.

Yet Heaven hath angels watching round
The Indian's lowliest forest-mound,—
And they have made it holy ground.

There ceases man's frail judgment; all
His powerless bolts of cursing fall
Unheeded on that grassy pall.

O peeled and hunted and reviled,
Sleep on, dark tenant of the wild!
Great Nature owns her simple child!

And Nature's God, to whom alone
The secret of the heart is known,—
The hidden language traced thereon;

Who from its many cumberings
Of form and creed, and outward things,
To light the naked spirit brings;

Not with our partial eye shall scan,
Not with our pride and scorn shall ban,
The spirit of our brother man!
1841.

ST. JOHN.

The fierce rivalry between Charles de La Tour, a Protestant, and D'Aulnay Charnasy, a Catholic, for the possession of Acadia, forms one of the most romantic passages in the history of the New World. La Tour received aid in several instances from the Puritan colony of Massachusetts. During one of his voyages for the purpose of obtaining arms and provisions for his establishment at St. John, his castle was attacked by D'Aulnay, and successfully defended by its high-spirited mistress. A second attack however followed in the fourth month, 1647, when D'Aulnay was successful, and the garrison was put to the sword. Lady La Tour languished a few days in the hands of her enemy, and then died of grief.

"To the winds give our banner!
Bear homeward again!"
Cried the Lord of Acadia,
Cried Charles of Estienne;
From the prow of his shallop
He gazed, as the sun,
From its bed in the ocean,
Streamed up the St. John.

O'er the blue western waters
That shallop had passed,
Where the mists of Penobscot
Clung damp on her mast.
St. Saviour had looked
On the heretic sail,
As the songs of the Huguenot
Rose on the gale.

The pale, ghostly fathers
Remembered her well,
And had cursed her while passing,
With taper and bell;
But the men of Monhegan,
Of Papists abhorred,
Had welcomed and feasted
The heretic Lord.

They had loaded his shallop
With dun-fish and ball,
With stores for his larder,
And steel for his wall.
Pemaquid, from her bastions

And turrets of stone,
Had welcomed his coming
With banner and gun.

And the prayers of the elders
Had followed his way,
As homeward he glided,
Down Pentecost Bay.
Oh, well sped La Tour
For, in peril and pain,
His lady kept watch,
For his coming again.

O'er the Isle of the Pheasant
The morning sun shone,
On the plane-trees which shaded
The shores of St. John.
"Now, why from yon battlements
Speaks not my love!
Why waves there no banner
My fortress above?"

Dark and wild, from his deck
St. Estienne gazed about,
On fire-wasted dwellings,
And silent redoubt;
From the low, shattered walls
Which the flame had o'errun,
There floated no banner,
There thundered no gun!

But beneath the low arch
Of its doorway there stood
A pale priest of Rome,
In his cloak and his hood.
With the bound of a lion,
La Tour sprang to land,
On the throat of the Papist
He fastened his hand.

"Speak, son of the Woman
Of scarlet and sin!
What wolf has been prowling
My castle within?"
From the grasp of the soldier
The Jesuit broke,

Half in scorn, half in sorrow,
He smiled as he spoke:

"No wolf, Lord of Estienne,
Has ravaged thy hall,
But thy red-handed rival,
With fire, steel, and ball!
On an errand of mercy
I hitherward came,
While the walls of thy castle
Yet spouted with flame.

"Pentagoet's dark vessels
Were moored in the bay,
Grim sea-lions, roaring
Aloud for their prey."
"But what of my lady?"
Cried Charles of Estienne.
"On the shot-crumbled turret
Thy lady was seen:

"Half-veiled in the smoke-cloud,
Her hand grasped thy pennon,
While her dark tresses swayed
In the hot breath of cannon!
But woe to the heretic,
Evermore woe!
When the son of the church
And the cross is his foe!

"In the track of the shell,
In the path of the ball,
Pentagoet swept over
The breach of the wall!
Steel to steel, gun to gun,
One moment,—and then
Alone stood the victor,
Alone with his men!

"Of its sturdy defenders,
Thy lady alone
Saw the cross-blazoned banner
Float over St. John."
"Let the dastard look to it!"
Cried fiery Estienne,

"Were D'Aulnay King Louis,
I'd free her again!"

"Alas for thy lady!
No service from thee
Is needed by her
Whom the Lord hath set free;
Nine days, in stern silence,
Her thraldom she bore,
But the tenth morning came,
And Death opened her door!"

As if suddenly smitten
La Tour staggered back;
His hand grasped his sword-hilt,
His forehead grew black.
He sprang on the deck
Of his shallop again.
"We cruise now for vengeance!
Give way!" cried Estienne.

"Massachusetts shall hear
Of the Huguenot's wrong,
And from island and creekside
Her fishers shall throng!
Pentagoet shall rue
What his Papists have done,
When his palisades echo
The Puritan's gun!"

Oh, the loveliest of heavens
Hung tenderly o'er him,
There were waves in the sunshine,
And green isles before him:
But a pale hand was beckoning
The Huguenot on;
And in blackness and ashes
Behind was St. John!
1841

THE CYPRESS-TREE OF CEYLON.

Ibn Batuta, the celebrated Mussulman traveller of the fourteenth century, speaks of a cypress-tree in Ceylon, universally held sacred by the natives, the leaves of which were said to fall only at certain intervals, and he who had the happiness to find and eat one of them was restored, at once, to youth and vigor. The traveller saw several venerable Jogees, or saints, sitting silent and motionless under the tree, patiently awaiting the falling of a leaf.

THEY sat in silent watchfulness
The sacred cypress-tree about,
And, from beneath old wrinkled brows,
Their failing eyes looked out.

Gray Age and Sickness waiting there
Through weary night and lingering day,—
Grim as the idols at their side,
And motionless as they.

Unheeded in the boughs above
The song of Ceylon's birds was sweet;
Unseen of them the island flowers
Bloomed brightly at their feet.

O'er them the tropic night-storm swept,
The thunder crashed on rock and hill;
The cloud-fire on their eyeballs blazed,
Yet there they waited still!

What was the world without to them?
The Moslem's sunset-call, the dance
Of Ceylon's maids, the passing gleam
Of battle-flag and lance?

They waited for that falling leaf
Of which the wandering Jogees sing:
Which lends once more to wintry age
The greenness of its spring.

Oh, if these poor and blinded ones
In trustful patience wait to feel
O'er torpid pulse and failing limb
A youthful freshness steal;

Shall we, who sit beneath that Tree
Whose healing leaves of life are shed,

In answer to the breath of prayer,
Upon the waiting head;

Not to restore our failing forms,
And build the spirit's broken shrine,
But on the fainting soul to shed
A light and life divine—

Shall we grow weary in our watch,
And murmur at the long delay?
Impatient of our Father's time
And His appointed way?

Or shall the stir of outward things
Allure and claim the Christian's eye,
When on the heathen watcher's ear
Their powerless murmurs die?

Alas! a deeper test of faith
Than prison cell or martyr's stake,
The self-abasing watchfulness
Of silent prayer may make.

We gird us bravely to rebuke
Our erring brother in the wrong,—
And in the ear of Pride and Power
Our warning voice is strong.

Easier to smite with Peter's sword
Than "watch one hour" in humbling prayer.
Life's "great things," like the Syrian lord,
Our hearts can do and dare.

But oh! we shrink from Jordan's side,
From waters which alone can save;

And murmur for Abana's banks
And Pharpar's brighter wave.

O Thou, who in the garden's shade
Didst wake Thy weary ones again,
Who slumbered at that fearful hour
Forgetful of Thy pain;

Bend o'er us now, as over them,
And set our sleep-bound spirits free,
Nor leave us slumbering in the watch

Our souls should keep with Thee!
1841

THE EXILES.

The incidents upon which the following ballad has its foundation about the year 1660. Thomas Macy was one of the first, if not the first white settler of Nantucket. The career of Macy is briefly but carefully outlined in James S. Pike's The New Puritan.

THE goodman sat beside his door
One sultry afternoon,
With his young wife singing at his side
An old and goodly tune.

A glimmer of heat was in the air,—
The dark green woods were still;
And the skirts of a heavy thunder-cloud
Hung over the western hill.

Black, thick, and vast arose that cloud
Above the wilderness,
As some dark world from upper air
Were stooping over this.

At times the solemn thunder pealed,
And all was still again,
Save a low murmur in the air
Of coming wind and rain.

Just as the first big rain-drop fell,
A weary stranger came,
And stood before the farmer's door,
With travel soiled and lame.

Sad seemed he, yet sustaining hope
Was in his quiet glance,
And peace, like autumn's moonlight, clothed
His tranquil countenance,—

A look, like that his Master wore
In Pilate's council-hall:
It told of wrongs, but of a love
Meekly forgiving all.

"Friend! wilt thou give me shelter here?"
The stranger meekly said;
And, leaning on his oaken staff,
The goodman's features read.

"My life is hunted,—evil men
Are following in my track;
The traces of the torturer's whip
Are on my aged back;

"And much, I fear, 't will peril thee
Within thy doors to take
A hunted seeker of the Truth,
Oppressed for conscience' sake."

Oh, kindly spoke the goodman's wife,
"Come in, old man!" quoth she,
"We will not leave thee to the storm,
Whoever thou mayst be."

Then came the aged wanderer in,
And silent sat him down;
While all within grew dark as night
Beneath the storm-cloud's frown.

But while the sudden lightning's blaze
Filled every cottage nook,
And with the jarring thunder-roll
The loosened casements shook,

A heavy tramp of horses' feet
Came sounding up the lane,
And half a score of horse, or more,
Came plunging through the rain.

"Now, Goodman Macy, ope thy door,—
We would not be house-breakers;
A rueful deed thou'st done this day,
In harboring banished Quakers."

Out looked the cautious goodman then,
With much of fear and awe,
For there, with broad wig drenched with rain
The parish priest he saw.

Open thy door, thou wicked man,
And let thy pastor in,
And give God thanks, if forty stripes
Repay thy deadly sin."

"What seek ye?" quoth the goodman;
"The stranger is my guest;

He is worn with toil and grievous wrong,—
Pray let the old man rest."

"Now, out upon thee, canting knave!"
And strong hands shook the door.
"Believe me, Macy," quoth the priest,
"Thou 'lt rue thy conduct sore."

Then kindled Macy's eye of fire
"No priest who walks the earth,
Shall pluck away the stranger-guest
Made welcome to my hearth."

Down from his cottage wall he caught
The matchlock, hotly tried
At Preston-pans and Marston-moor,
By fiery Ireton's side;

Where Puritan, and Cavalier,
With shout and psalm contended;
And Rupert's oath, and Cromwell's prayer,
With battle-thunder blended.

Up rose the ancient stranger then
"My spirit is not free
To bring the wrath and violence
Of evil men on thee;

"And for thyself, I pray forbear,
Bethink thee of thy Lord,
Who healed again the smitten ear,
And sheathed His follower's sword.

"I go, as to the slaughter led.
Friends of the poor, farewell!"
Beneath his hand the oaken door
Back on its hinges fell.

"Come forth, old graybeard, yea and nay,"
The reckless scoffers cried,
As to a horseman's saddle-bow
The old man's arms were tied.

And of his bondage hard and long
In Boston's crowded jail,
Where suffering woman's prayer was heard,
With sickening childhood's wail,

It suits not with our tale to tell;
Those scenes have passed away;
Let the dim shadows of the past
Brood o'er that evil day.

"Ho, sheriff!" quoth the ardent priest,
"Take Goodman Macy too;
The sin of this day's heresy
His back or purse shall rue."

"Now, goodwife, haste thee!" Macy cried.
She caught his manly arm;
Behind, the parson urged pursuit,
With outcry and alarm.

Ho! speed the Macys, neck or naught,—
The river-course was near;
The plashing on its pebbled shore
Was music to their ear.

A gray rock, tasselled o'er with birch,
Above the waters hung,
And at its base, with every wave,
A small light wherry swung.

A leap—they gain the boat—and there
The goodman wields his oar;
"Ill luck betide them all," he cried,
"The laggards on the shore."

Down through the crashing underwood,
The burly sheriff came:—
"Stand, Goodman Macy, yield thyself;
Yield in the King's own name."

"Now out upon thy hangman's face!"
Bold Macy answered then,—
"Whip women, on the village green,
But meddle not with men."

The priest came panting to the shore,
His grave cocked hat was gone;
Behind him, like some owl's nest, hung
His wig upon a thorn.

"Come back,—come back!" the parson cried,
"The church's curse beware."

"Curse, an' thou wilt," said Macy, "but
Thy blessing prithee spare."

"Vile scoffer!" cried the baffled priest,
"Thou 'lt yet the gallows see."
"Who's born to be hanged will not be drowned,"
Quoth Macy, merrily;

"And so, sir sheriff and priest, good-by!"
He bent him to his oar,
And the small boat glided quietly
From the twain upon the shore.

Now in the west, the heavy clouds
Scattered and fell asunder,
While feebler came the rush of rain,
And fainter growled the thunder.

And through the broken clouds, the sun
Looked out serene and warm,
Painting its holy symbol-light
Upon the passing storm.

Oh, beautiful! that rainbow span,
O'er dim Crane-neck was bended;
One bright foot touched the eastern hills,
And one with ocean blended.

By green Pentucket's southern'slope
The small boat glided fast;
The watchers of the Block-house saw
The strangers as they passed.

That night a stalwart garrison
Sat shaking in their shoes,
To hear the dip of Indian oars,
The glide of birch canoes.

The fisher-wives of Salisbury—
The men were all away—
Looked out to see the stranger oar
Upon their waters play.

Deer-Island's rocks and fir-trees threw
Their sunset-shadows o'er them,
And Newbury's spire and weathercock
Peered o'er the pines before them.

Around the Black Rocks, on their left,
The marsh lay broad and green;
And on their right, with dwarf shrubs crowned,
Plum Island's hills were seen.

With skilful hand and wary eye
The harbor-bar was crossed;
A plaything of the restless wave,
The boat on ocean tossed.

The glory of the sunset heaven
On land and water lay;
On the steep hills of Agawam,
On cape, and bluff, and bay.

They passed the gray rocks of Cape Ann,
And Gloucester's harbor-bar;
The watch-fire of the garrison
Shone like a setting star.

How brightly broke the morning
On Massachusetts Bay!
Blue wave, and bright green island,
Rejoicing in the day.

On passed the bark in safety
Round isle and headland steep;
No tempest broke above them,
No fog-cloud veiled the deep.

Far round the bleak and stormy Cape
The venturous Macy passed,
And on Nantucket's naked isle
Drew up his boat at last.

And how, in log-built cabin,
They braved the rough sea-weather;
And there, in peace and quietness,
Went down life's vale together;

How others drew around them,
And how their fishing sped,
Until to every wind of heaven
Nantucket's sails were spread;

How pale Want alternated
With Plenty's golden smile;

Behold, is it not written
In the annals of the isle?

And yet that isle remaineth
A refuge of the free,
As when true-hearted Macy
Beheld it from the sea.

Free as the winds that winnow
Her shrubless hills of sand,
Free as the waves that batter
Along her yielding land.

Than hers, at duty's summons,
No loftier spirit stirs,
Nor falls o'er human suffering
A readier tear then hers.

God bless the sea-beat island!
And grant forevermore,
That charity and freedom dwell
As now upon her shore!
1841.

THE KNIGHT OF ST. JOHN.

ERE down yon blue Carpathian hills
The sun shall sink again,
Farewell to life and all its ills,
Farewell to cell and chain!

These prison shades are dark and cold,
But, darker far than they,
The shadow of a sorrow old
Is on my heart alway.

For since the day when Warkworth wood
Closed o'er my steed, and I,
An alien from my name and blood,
A weed cast out to die,—

When, looking back in sunset light,
I saw her turret gleam,
And from its casement, far and white,
Her sign of farewell stream,

Like one who, from some desert shore,
Doth home's green isles descry,
And, vainly longing, gazes o'er
The waste of wave and sky;

So from the desert of my fate
I gaze across the past;
Forever on life's dial-plate
The shade is backward cast!

I've wandered wide from shore to shore,
I've knelt at many a shrine;
And bowed me to the rocky floor
Where Bethlehem's tapers shine;

And by the Holy Sepulchre
I've pledged my knightly sword
To Christ, His blessed Church, and her,
The Mother of our Lord.

Oh, vain the vow, and vain the strife!
How vain do all things seem!
My soul is in the past, and life
To-day is but a dream.

In vain the penance strange and long,
And hard for flesh to bear;
The prayer, the fasting, and the thong,
And sackcloth shirt of hair.

The eyes of memory will not sleep,
Its ears are open still;
And vigils with the past they keep
Against my feeble will.

And still the loves and joys of old
Do evermore uprise;
I see the flow of locks of gold,
The shine of loving eyes!

Ah me! upon another's breast
Those golden locks recline;
I see upon another rest
The glance that once was mine.

"O faithless priest! O perjured knight!"
I hear the Master cry;
"Shut out the vision from thy sight,
Let Earth and Nature die.

"The Church of God is now thy spouse,
And thou the bridegroom art;
Then let the burden of thy vows
Crush down thy human heart!"

In vain! This heart its grief must know,
Till life itself hath ceased,
And falls beneath the self-same blow
The lover and the priest!

O pitying Mother! souls of light,
And saints and martyrs old!
Pray for a weak and sinful knight,
A suffering man uphold.

Then let the Paynim work his will,
And death unbind my chain,
Ere down yon blue Carpathian hill
The sun shall fall again.
1843

CASSANDRA SOUTHWICK. In 1658 two young persons, son and daughter of Lawrence Smithwick of Salem, who had himself been imprisoned and deprived of nearly all his property for having entertained Quakers at his house, were fined for non-attendance at church. They being unable to pay the fine, the General Court issued an order empowering "the Treasurer of the County to sell the said persons to any of the English nation of Virginia or Barbadoes, to answer said fines." An attempt was made to carry this order into execution, but no shipmaster was found willing to convey them to the West Indies.

To the God of all sure mercies let my blessing rise
to-day,
From the scoffer and the cruel He hath plucked
the spoil away;
Yea, He who cooled the furnace around the faithful
three,
And tamed the Chaldean lions, hath set His handmaid free!
Last night I saw the sunset melt through my prison
bars,
Last night across my damp earth-floor fell the pale
gleam of stars;
In the coldness and the darkness all through the
long night-time,
My grated casement whitened with autumn's early
rime.
Alone, in that dark sorrow, hour after hour crept
by;
Star after star looked palely in and sank adown
the sky;
No sound amid night's stillness, save that which
seemed to be
The dull and heavy beating of the pulses of the sea;

All night I sat unsleeping, for I knew that on the
morrow
The ruler and the cruel priest would mock me in
my sorrow,
Dragged to their place of market, and bargained
for and sold,
Like a lamb before the shambles, like a heifer
from the fold!

Oh, the weakness of the flesh was there, the
shrinking and the shame;
And the low voice of the Tempter like whispers to
me came:

"Why sit'st thou thus forlornly," the wicked murmur said,
"Damp walls thy bower of beauty, cold earth thy maiden bed?

"Where be the smiling faces, and voices soft and sweet,
Seen in thy father's dwelling, heard in the pleasant street?
Where be the youths whose glances, the summer Sabbath through,
Turned tenderly and timidly unto thy father's pew?

"Why sit'st thou here, Cassandra?-Bethink thee with what mirth Thy happy schoolmates gather around the warm bright hearth; How the crimson shadows tremble on foreheads white and fair, On eyes of merry girlhood, half hid in golden hair.

"Not for thee the hearth-fire brightens, not for thee kind words are spoken,
Not for thee the nuts of Wenham woods by laughing boys are broken;
No first-fruits of the orchard within thy lap are laid,
For thee no flowers of autumn the youthful hunters braid.

"O weak, deluded maiden!—by crazy fancies led,
With wild and raving railers an evil path to tread;
To leave a wholesome worship, and teaching pure and sound,
And mate with maniac women, loose-haired and sackcloth bound,—

"Mad scoffers of the priesthood; who mock at things divine,
Who rail against the pulpit, and holy bread and wine;
Sore from their cart-tail scourgings, and from the pillory lame,
Rejoicing in their wretchedness, and glorying in their shame.

"And what a fate awaits thee!—a sadly toiling slave,

Dragging the slowly lengthening chain of bondage to the grave!
Think of thy woman's nature, subdued in hopeless thrall,
The easy prey of any, the scoff and scorn of all!"

Oh, ever as the Tempter spoke, and feeble Nature's fears
Wrung drop by drop the scalding flow of unavailing tears,
I wrestled down the evil thoughts, and strove in silent prayer,
To feel, O Helper of the weak! that Thou indeed wert there!

I thought of Paul and Silas, within Philippi's cell,
And how from Peter's sleeping limbs the prison shackles fell,
Till I seemed to hear the trailing of an angel's robe of white,
And to feel a blessed presence invisible to sight.

Bless the Lord for all his mercies!—for the peace and love I felt,
Like dew of Hermon's holy hill, upon my spirit melt;
When "Get behind me, Satan!" was the language of my heart,
And I felt the Evil Tempter with all his doubts depart.

Slow broke the gray cold morning; again the sunshine fell,
Flecked with the shade of bar and grate within my lonely cell;
The hoar-frost melted on the wall, and upward from the street
Came careless laugh and idle word, and tread of passing feet.

At length the heavy bolts fell back, my door was open cast,
And slowly at the sheriff's side, up the long street I passed;
I heard the murmur round me, and felt, but dared not see,

How, from every door and window, the people gazed on me.

And doubt and fear fell on me, shame burned upon my cheek,
Swam earth and sky around me, my trembling limbs grew weak:
"O Lord! support thy handmaid; and from her soul cast out
The fear of man, which brings a snare, the weakness and the doubt."

Then the dreary shadows scattered, like a cloud in morning's breeze,
And a low deep voice within me seemed whispering words like these:
"Though thy earth be as the iron, and thy heaven a brazen wall,
Trust still His loving-kindness whose power is over all."

We paused at length, where at my feet the sunlit waters broke
On glaring reach of shining beach, and shingly wall of rock;
The merchant-ships lay idly there, in hard clear lines on high,
Tracing with rope and slender spar their network on the sky.

And there were ancient citizens, cloak-wrapped and grave and cold,
And grim and stout sea-captains with faces bronzed and old,
And on his horse, with Rawson, his cruel clerk at hand,
Sat dark and haughty Endicott, the ruler of the land.

And poisoning with his evil words the ruler's ready ear,
The priest leaned o'er his saddle, with laugh and scoff and jeer;
It stirred my soul, and from my lips the seal of silence broke,

As if through woman's weakness a warning spirit spoke.

I cried, "The Lord rebuke thee, thou smiter of the meek,
Thou robber of the righteous, thou trampler of the weak!
Go light the dark, cold hearth-stones,—go turn the prison lock
Of the poor hearts thou hast hunted, thou wolf amid the flock!"

Dark lowered the brows of Endicott, and with a deeper red
O'er Rawson's wine-empurpled cheek the flush of anger spread;
"Good people," quoth the white-lipped priest, "heed not her words so wild,
Her Master speaks within her,—the Devil owns his child!"

But gray heads shook, and young brows knit, the while the sheriff read
That law the wicked rulers against the poor have made,
Who to their house of Rimmon and idol priesthood bring
No bended knee of worship, nor gainful offering.

Then to the stout sea-captains the sheriff, turning, said,—
"Which of ye, worthy seamen, will take this Quaker maid?
In the Isle of fair Barbadoes, or on Virginia's shore,
You may hold her at a higher price than Indian girl or Moor."

Grim and silent stood the captains; and when again he cried,
"Speak out, my worthy seamen!"—no voice, no sign replied;
But I felt a hard hand press my own, and kind words met my ear,—
"God bless thee, and preserve thee, my gentle girl and dear!"

A weight seemed lifted from my heart, a pitying friend was nigh,—
I felt it in his hard, rough hand, and saw it in his eye;
And when again the sheriff spoke, that voice, so kind to me,
Growled back its stormy answer like the roaring of the sea,—

"Pile my ship with bars of silver, pack with coins of Spanish gold,
From keel-piece up to deck-plank, the roomage of her hold,
By the living God who made me!—I would sooner in your bay
Sink ship and crew and cargo, than bear this child away!"

"Well answered, worthy captain, shame on their cruel laws!"
Ran through the crowd in murmurs loud the people's just applause.
"Like the herdsman of Tekoa, in Israel of old,
Shall we see the poor and righteous again for silver sold?"

I looked on haughty Endicott; with weapon half-way drawn,
Swept round the throng his lion glare of bitter hate and scorn;
Fiercely he drew his bridle-rein, and turned in silence back,
And sneering priest and baffled clerk rode murmuring in his track.

Hard after them the sheriff looked, in bitterness of soul; Thrice smote his staff upon the ground, and crushed his parchment roll. "Good friends," he said, "since both have fled, the ruler and the priest, Judge ye, if from their further work I be not well released."

Loud was the cheer which, full and clear, swept round the silent bay,
As, with kind words and kinder looks, he bade me go my way;
For He who turns the courses of the streamlet of the glen,

And the river of great waters, had turned the
hearts of men.

Oh, at that hour the very earth seemed changed
beneath my eye,
A holier wonder round me rose the blue walls of
the sky,
A lovelier light on rock and hill and stream and
woodland lay,
And softer lapsed on sunnier sands the waters of
the bay.
Thanksgiving to the Lord of life! to Him all
praises be,
Who from the hands of evil men hath set his handmaid free;
All praise to Him before whose power the mighty
are afraid,
Who takes the crafty in the snare which for the
poor is laid!
Sing, O my soul, rejoicingly, on evening's twilight
calm
Uplift the loud thanksgiving, pour forth the grateful
psalm;
Let all dear hearts with me rejoice, as did the
saints of old,
When of the Lord's good angel the rescued Peter
told.
And weep and howl, ye evil priests and mighty
men of wrong,
The Lord shall smite the proud, and lay His hand
upon the strong.
Woe to the wicked rulers in His avenging hour!
Woe to the wolves who seek the flocks to raven
and devour!

But let the humble ones arise, the poor in heart
be glad,
And let the mourning ones again with robes of
praise be clad.
For He who cooled the furnace, and smoothed the
stormy wave,
And tamed the Chaldean lions, is mighty still to
save!
1843.

THE NEW WIFE AND THE OLD.

The following ballad is founded upon one of the marvellous legends connected with the famous General ———, of Hampton, New Hampshire, who was regarded by his neighbors as a Yankee Faust, in league with the adversary. I give the story, as I heard it when a child, from a venerable family visitant.

DARK the halls, and cold the feast,
Gone the bridemaids, gone the priest.
All is over, all is done,
Twain of yesterday are one!
Blooming girl and manhood gray,
Autumn in the arms of May!

Hushed within and hushed without,
Dancing feet and wrestlers' shout;
Dies the bonfire on the hill;
All is dark and all is still,
Save the starlight, save the breeze
Moaning through the graveyard trees,
And the great sea-waves below,
Pulse of the midnight beating slow.

From the brief dream of a bride
She hath wakened, at his side.
With half-uttered shriek and start,—
Feels she not his beating heart?
And the pressure of his arm,
And his breathing near and warm?

Lightly from the bridal bed
Springs that fair dishevelled head,
And a feeling, new, intense,
Half of shame, half innocence,
Maiden fear and wonder speaks
Through her lips and changing cheeks.

From the oaken mantel glowing,
Faintest light the lamp is throwing
On the mirror's antique mould,
High-backed chair, and wainscot old,
And, through faded curtains stealing,
His dark sleeping face revealing.

Listless lies the strong man there,
Silver-streaked his careless hair;
Lips of love have left no trace
On that hard and haughty face;
And that forehead's knitted thought
Love's soft hand hath not unwrought.

"Yet," she sighs, "he loves me well,
More than these calm lips will tell.
Stooping to my lowly state,
He hath made me rich and great,
And I bless him, though he be
Hard and stern to all save me!"

While she speaketh, falls the light
O'er her fingers small and white;
Gold and gem, and costly ring
Back the timid lustre fling,—
Love's selectest gifts, and rare,
His proud hand had fastened there.

Gratefully she marks the glow
From those tapering lines of snow;
Fondly o'er the sleeper bending
His black hair with golden blending,
In her soft and light caress,
Cheek and lip together press.

Ha!—that start of horror! why
That wild stare and wilder cry,
Full of terror, full of pain?
Is there madness in her brain?
Hark! that gasping, hoarse and low,
"Spare me,—spare me,—let me go!"

God have mercy!—icy cold
Spectral hands her own enfold,
Drawing silently from them
Love's fair gifts of gold and gem.
"Waken! save me!" still as death
At her side he slumbereth.

Ring and bracelet all are gone,
And that ice-cold hand withdrawn;
But she hears a murmur low,
Full of sweetness, full of woe,

Half a sigh and half a moan
"Fear not! give the dead her own!"

Ah!—the dead wife's voice she knows!
That cold hand whose pressure froze,
Once in warmest life had borne
Gem and band her own hath worn.
"Wake thee! wake thee!" Lo, his eyes
Open with a dull surprise.

In his arms the strong man folds her,
Closer to his breast he holds her;
Trembling limbs his own are meeting,
And he feels her heart's quick beating
"Nay, my dearest, why this fear?"
"Hush!" she saith, "the dead is here!"

"Nay, a dream,—an idle dream."
But before the lamp's pale gleam
Tremblingly her hand she raises.
There no more the diamond blazes,
Clasp of pearl, or ring of gold,—
"Ah!" she sighs, "her hand was cold!"

Broken words of cheer he saith,
But his dark lip quivereth,
And as o'er the past he thinketh,
From his young wife's arms he shrinketh;
Can those soft arms round him lie,
Underneath his dead wife's eye?

She her fair young head can rest
Soothed and childlike on his breast,
And in trustful innocence
Draw new strength and courage thence;
He, the proud man, feels within
But the cowardice of sin!

She can murmur in her thought
Simple prayers her mother taught,
And His blessed angels call,
Whose great love is over all;
He, alone, in prayerless pride,
Meets the dark Past at her side!

One, who living shrank with dread
From his look, or word, or tread,

Unto whom her early grave
Was as freedom to the slave,
Moves him at this midnight hour,
With the dead's unconscious power!

Ah, the dead, the unforgot!
From their solemn homes of thought,
Where the cypress shadows blend
Darkly over foe and friend,
Or in love or sad rebuke,
Back upon the living look.

And the tenderest ones and weakest,
Who their wrongs have borne the meekest,
Lifting from those dark, still places,
Sweet and sad-remembered faces,
O'er the guilty hearts behind
An unwitting triumph find.

1843